IN TUNE WITH
THE INFINITE

IN TUNE WITH THE INFINITE

The Timeless Classic on the Power of Your Eternal Mind

Ralph Waldo Trine

Abridged and Introduced
by Mitch Horowitz

THE CONDENSED CLASSICS LIBRARY™

Published by Gildan Media LLC
aka G&D Media.
www.GandDmedia.com

In Tune With the Infinite was originally published in 1897

G&D Media Condensed Classics edition published 2021

Abridgement and Introduction copyright © 2021 by Mitch Horowitz

FIRST PRINT AND EBOOK EDITION: 2021

Cover design by David Rheinhardt of Pyrographx

Interior design by Meghan Day Healey of Story Horse, LLC.

ISBN: 978-1-7225-0076-4

Contents

Bringing the Infinite to Earth

by Mitch Horowitz

In one of my favorite scenes from *The Wizard of Oz* Dorothy is running away from home and happens upon the wagon of a Professor Marvel who sympathetically invites her inside to his fortunetelling parlor. Seating Dorothy before a crystal ball, Professor Marvel tells the wide-eyed girl:

> *That's right. Here—sit right down here. That's it. Ha ha! This—this is the same genuine, magic, authentic crystal used by the Priests of Isis and Osiris in the days of the Pharaohs of Egypt—in which Cleopatra first saw the approach of Julius Caesar and Marc Antony, and—and so on— and so on. Now, you—you'd better close your*

eyes, my child, for a moment—in order to be better in tune with the infinite.

In tune with the infinite. The title of Ralph Waldo Trine's 1897 book retained posterity as a catchphrase for numinous realities in the 1939 movie, more than a generation after its publication. (Neither the scene nor phrase appears in Theosophist L. Frank Baum's original novel from 1900.) The reference testifies to the enormity of the book's cultural reach and recognition in the first half of the twentieth century. In many respects, *In Tune With the Infinite* was the nation's first mass bestseller of therapeutic spirituality, laying the template for future works such as *Alcoholics Anonymous* in 1939 and Norman Vincent Peale's *The Power of Positive Thinking* in 1952, both of which use Trine's phraseology, if not always with attribution.

Although the *Oz* screenwriters were poking gentle fun at the author, the movie also presented the perfect framing of Trine's metaphysics, which echoed and augmented the popular spiritual vision of the nation itself: belief in the innocence of the individual, the capacity to break through to other realms, and the transcendent promise of self-improvement.

Indeed, many of Trine's phrases and themes entered the lexicon of American spirituality. The term

"Higher Power"—central to Alcoholics Anonymous and the 12-step movement—probably came from *In Tune With the Infinite*, where Trine repeatedly used the phrase with particular reference to alcohol: "In the degree that we come into the realization of the higher powers of the mind and spirit . . . there also falls away the desire for the heavier, grosser, less valuable kinds of food and drink, such as the flesh of animals, alcoholic drinks . . ." Trine helped popularize the term "Law of Attraction," which until his book was a little-known phrase from deep within the folds of metaphysical culture (and was only just coming into coinage for the concept of like thoughts attracting like circumstances). Many writers, including Neville Goddard, adopted Trine's term "enter the silence" to signal communion with the infinite. William James mentioned Trine as among the New Thought figures who moved him to conclude that "it really looks as if a good start might be made in the direction of changing our American mental habit into something more indifferent and strong." (By *indifferent* James meant serviceable and utilitarian.) Henry Ford called the book a major factor in his success and pressed copies on friends and visitors to his office. Even televangelist Oral Roberts echoed Trine, encouraging readers to reflect: "I am in tune with God."

———

The man who started it all was born in Northern Illinois in 1866, the same year as the death of mental-healing pioneer Phineas Quimby. Ralph Waldo Trine, named for Transcendentalist philosopher Ralph Waldo Emerson, studied history and political science at Johns Hopkins University and later won a $100 prize for an essay on "The Effects of Humane Education on the Prevention of Crime." Little is known about Trine personally, including the mystical influences that led to his signature work soon after he turned 31. What is evident is that beneath the placid, almost priestly exterior that appears in his photographs burned a desire to unite mysticism and social reform. A 1902 profile in the New Thought magazine *Mind* said that Trine believed in the cooperative ethos of socialism and that he planned to write a book "from the viewpoint of a socialist who is such because of his New Thought philosophy."

It is not clear that Trine ever wrote such a book, but something very close appeared under his byline in 1910: *Land of Living Men.* While *In Tune With the Infinite* employed a gentle, folksy tone emphasizing gratitude and generosity, *Land of Living Men* revealed different colors. The New Thought pioneer called for "a great people's movement to bring back to the people the immense belongings that have been taken away from them." Trine advocated busting up monopolies, striking for higher wages, and placing essential utilities and industries into public hands. This was one book that Henry Ford didn't give away to friends. In fact, *Land of Living Men* seemed to make little impact at all on Trine's followers. By 1928, Trine was an honored guest in Ford's office, where he engaged in an almost fawning interview with the automaker. Their conversation was turned into a popular book, *The Power That Wins,* which ranged from Ford's love for avocados to his belief in reincarnation. Whatever Trine's innermost commitments, he would never again be seen—nor succeed as—a political Jeremiah.

The power of *In Tune With the Infinite* rests on two counts. The first is that Trine created perhaps not the earliest but the most effective and widely accessible iteration of the New Thought gospel that thoughts are causative. Trine's popularization remained unmatched until Norman Vincent Peale published *The Power of Positive Thinking* more than fifty years later. But Trine's book was something that Peale's was not—and this forms the second basis of its achievement. Although Trine's reference points are chiefly Christian, *In Tune*

With the Infinite is one of the first widely popular works of *religious universalism*.

Peale's book was explicitly Christian; the Dutch Reform minister reimagined New Thought in language that was reassuringly familiar to the church-going public. (Although even in this regard Peale snuck in some radically mystical concepts and references.) Trine, by contrast, incorporated principles, if not always language, from broad-spanning religious traditions. In some respects, *In Tune With the Infinite* is as much a popularization of New Thought as it is of Hermetic philosophy. Hermeticism is a late-ancient Greek-Egyptian mystical school that taught that the individual is an extension of a higher mind, or *Nous*, and possesses the same creative potentials. You'll see this on display in chapter three, "The Supreme Fact of Human Life," where Trine talks about the nature of the "God-man." In chapter four, "Fullness of Life—Bodily Health and Vigor," Trine remakes the core Hermetic dictum "As above, so below" into "As within, so without; cause, effect." The Hermetic outlook is likewise present when Trine talks about a "divine inflow" into the individual. This also echoes eighteenth-century mystic Emanuel Swedenborg's concept of a "Divine influx."

Trine, for all his folksy language, was a radical thinker. And *In Tune With the Infinite*, a book that ultimately sold more than two million copies when the nation itself was far less populous than today, brought everyday Americans ideas that were jarring, fresh, anti-mainstream, and transcendent. That such themes of spiritual possibility sound so familiar to us today is testament to the author's legacy.

There is a golden thread that runs through every religion in the world. There is a golden thread that runs through the lives and the teachings of all the prophets, seers, sages, and saviors in the world's history, through the lives of all men and women of truly great and lasting power. All that they have ever done or attained to has been done in full accordance with law. What one has done, all may do.

This same golden thread must enter into the lives of all who today, in this busy work-a-day world of ours, would exchange impotence for power, weakness and suffering for abounding health and strength, pain and unrest for perfect peace, poverty of whatever nature for fullness and plenty.

Each is building his own world. We both build from within and we attract from without. Thought is the force with which we build, for thoughts are forces.

Like builds like and like attracts like. In the degree that thought is spiritualized does it become more subtle and powerful in its workings. This spiritualizing is in accordance with law and is within the power of all.

Everything is first worked out in the unseen before it is manifested in the seen, in the ideal before it is realized in the real, in the spiritual before it shows forth in the material. The realm of the unseen is the realm of cause. The realm of the seen is the realm of effect. The nature of effect is always determined and conditioned by the nature of its cause.

There is a divine sequence running throughout the universe. Within and above and below the human will incessantly works the Divine will. To come into harmony with it and thereby with all the higher laws and forces, to come then into league and to work in conjunction with them, in order that they can work in league and in conjunction with us, is to come into the chain of this wonderful sequence. This is the secret of all success.

Chapter One

Fullness of Peace, Power and Plenty

The optimist is right. The pessimist is right. The one differs from the other as the light from the dark. Yet both are right. Each is right from his own particular point of view, and this point of view is the determining factor in the life of each. It determines as to whether it is a life of power or of impotence, of peace or of pain, of success or of failure.

The optimist has the power of seeing things in their entirety and in their right relations. The pessimist looks from a limited and a one-sided point of view. The one has his understanding illumined by wisdom, the understanding of the other is darkened by ignorance. Each is building his world from within, and the result of the building is determined by the point of view of each. The optimist, by his superior wisdom and insight, is making his own heaven, and in the degree that he makes his own heaven is he helping to make one for all the world beside. The pessimist, by virtue of his limitations, is making his own hell, and in the degree that he makes his own hell is he helping to make one for all mankind.

You and I have the predominating characteristics of an optimist or the predominating characteristics of a pessimist. We then are making, hour by hour, our own heaven or our own hell; and in the degree that we are making the one or the other for ourselves are we helping make it for all the world beside.

CHAPTER TWO

The Supreme Fact
of the Universe

The great central fact of the universe is that Spirit of Infinite Life and Power is behind all, animates all, manifests itself in and through all; that self-existent principle of life is that from which all has come, and not only from which all has come, but from which all is continually coming. If there is an individual life, there must of necessity be an infinite source of life from which it comes. If there is a quality or a force of love, there must of necessity be an infinite source of love whence it comes. If there is wisdom, there must be the all-wise source behind it from which it springs. The same is true in regard to peace, the same in regard to power, the same in regard to what we call material things.

There is, then, this Spirit of Infinite Life and Power behind all, which is the source of all. This Infinite

Power is creating, working, ruling through the agency of great immutable laws and forces that run through all the universe, that surround us on every side. Every act of our every-day lives is governed by these same great laws and forces. Every flower that blooms by the wayside, springs up, grows, blooms, fades, according to certain great immutable laws. Every snowflake that plays between earth and heaven, forms, falls, melts, according to certain great unchangeable laws.

In a sense there is nothing in all the great universe but law. If this is true there must of necessity be a force behind it all that is the maker of these laws and a force greater than the laws that are made. This Spirit of Infinite Life and Power that is behind all is what I call God. I care not what term you may use, be it Kindly Light, Providence, the Over Soul, Omnipotence, or whatever term may be most convenient. I care not what the term may be as long as we are agreed in regard to the great central fact itself.

God, then, is this Infinite Spirit which fills all the universe with Himself alone, so that all is from Him and in Him, and there is nothing that is outside. Indeed and in truth, then, in Him we live and move and have our being. He is the life of our life, our very life itself. We have received, we are continually receiving our life from Him. We are partakers of the life of God; and though we differ from Him in that we are individualized spirits, while He is the Infinite Spirit including us as well as all else beside, yet *in essence the life of God and the life of man are identically the same, and so are one.* They differ not in essence, in quality; they differ in degree.

There have been and are highly illumined souls who believe that we receive our life from God after the manner of a divine inflow. And again, there have been and are those who believe that our life is one with the life of God, and so that God and man are one. Which is right? Both are right; both right when rightly understood.

In regard to the first: if God is the Infinite Spirit of Life behind all, whence all comes, then clearly our life as individualized spirits is continually coming from this Infinite Source by means of this divine inflow. In the second place, if our lives as individualized spirits are directly from, are parts of this Infinite Spirit of Life, then the degree of the Infinite Spirit that is manifested in the life of each must be identical in quality with that Source, the same as a drop of water taken from the ocean is, in nature, in characteristics, identical with that ocean, its source. And how could it be otherwise? The liability to misunderstanding in this latter case, however, is this: in that although the life of God and the life of man in essence are identically the same, the life of God so far transcends the life of individual man that it includes all else beside. In other words, so far as the quality of life is concerned, in essence they are the same; so far as the degree of life is concerned, they are vastly different.

There is a reservoir in a valley which receives its supply from an inexhaustible reservoir on the mountain side. It is then true that the reservoir in the valley receives its supply by virtue of the inflow of the water from the larger reservoir on the mountain side. It is also true that the water in this smaller reservoir is in nature, in quality, in characteristics identically the same as that in the larger reservoir which is its source. The difference, however, is this: the reservoir on the mountain side, in the *amount* of its water, so far transcends the reservoir in the valley that it can supply an innumerable number of like reservoirs and still be unexhausted.

If this is true, does it not then follow that in the degree that man opens himself to this divine inflow does he approach to God? If so, it then necessarily follows that in the degree that he makes this approach does he take on the God-powers. And if the God-powers are without limit, does it not then follow that the only limitations man has are the limitations he sets to himself, by virtue of not knowing himself?

Chapter Three

The Supreme Fact
of Human Life

From the great central fact of the universe in regard to which we have agreed, namely, this Spirit of Infinite Life that is behind all and from which all comes, we are led to inquire as to what is the great central fact in human life. From what has gone before, the question almost answers itself.

The great central fact in human life, in your life and in mine, is the coming into a conscious, vital realization of our oneness with this Infinite Life, and the opening of ourselves fully to this divine inflow. This is the great central fact in human life, for in this all else is included, all else follows in its train. In just the degree that we come into a conscious realization of our oneness with the Infinite Life, and open ourselves to this divine inflow, do we actualize in ourselves the qualities and powers of the Infinite Life.

And what does this mean? It means simply this: that we are recognizing our true identity, that we are bringing our lives into harmony with the same great laws and forces, and so opening ourselves to the same great inspirations, as have all the prophets, seers, sages, and saviors in the world's history, all men of truly great and mighty power. For in the degree that we come into this realization and connect ourselves with this Infinite Source, do we make it possible for the higher powers to play, to work, to manifest through us.

We can keep closed to this divine inflow, to these higher forces and powers, through ignorance, as most of us do, and thus hinder or even prevent their manifesting through us. Or we can intentionally close ourselves to their operations and thus deprive ourselves of the powers to which, by the very nature of our being, we are rightful heirs. On the other hand, we can come into so vital a realization of the oneness of our real selves with this Infinite Life, and can open ourselves so fully to the incoming of this divine inflow, and so to the operation of these higher forces, inspirations, and powers, that we can indeed and in truth become what we may well term, God-men.

And what is a God-man? One in whom the powers of God are manifesting, though yet a man. No one can set limitations to a man or a woman of this type; for the only limitations he or she can have are those set by the self. Ignorance is the most potent factor in setting limitations to the majority of mankind; and so the great majority of people continue to live their little, dwarfed, and stunted lives simply by virtue of the fact that they do not realize the larger life to which they are heirs. They have never as yet come into a knowledge of the real identity of their true selves.

Mankind has not yet realized that the real self is one with the life of God. Through its ignorance it has never yet opened itself to the divine inflow, and so has never made itself a channel through which the infinite powers and forces can manifest. When we know ourselves merely as men, we live accordingly, and have merely the powers of men. When we come into the realization of the fact that we are God-men, then again we live accordingly, and have the powers of God-men. *In the degree that we open ourselves to this divine inflow are we changed from mere men into God-men.*

Before we proceed farther let us consider very briefly the nature of thought. Thought is not, as is many times supposed, a mere indefinite abstraction, or something of a like nature. It is, on the contrary, a vital, living force, the most vital, subtle, and irresistible force there is in the universe.

Everything in the material universe about us, everything the universe has ever known, had its origin first in thought. From this it took its form. Every castle, every statue, every painting, every piece of mechanism, everything had its birth, its origin, first in the mind of the one who formed it before it received its material expression or embodiment. The very universe in which we live is the result of the thought energies of God, the Infinite Spirit that is back of all. And if it is true, as we have found, that we in our true selves are in essence the same, and in this sense are one with the life of this Infinite Spirit, do we not then see that in the degree that we come into a vital realization of this stupendous fact, *we, through the operation of our interior, spiritual, thought forces, have in like sense creative power?*

Everything exists in the unseen before it is manifested or realized in the seen, and in this sense it is true that the unseen things are the real, while the things that are seen are the unreal. The unseen things are *cause*; the seen things are *effect*. The unseen things are the eternal; the seen things are the changing, the transient.

Much is said in regard to "building castles in the air," and one who is given to this building is not always looked upon with favor. But castles in the air are always necessary before we can have castles on the ground, before we can have castles in which to live. The trouble with the one who gives himself to building castles in the air is not that he builds them in the air, but that he does not go farther and actualize in life, in character, in material form, the castles he thus builds. He does a part of the work, a very necessary part; but another equally necessary part remains still undone.

There is in connection with the thought forces what we may term, the drawing power of mind, and the great law operating here is one with that great law of the universe, that like attracts like. We are continually attracting to us from both the seen and the unseen side of life, forces and conditions most akin to those of our own thoughts.

This law is continually operating whether we are conscious of it or not. We are all living, so to speak, in a vast ocean of thought, and the very atmosphere around us is continually filled with the thought forces that are being continually sent or that are continually going out in the form of thought waves. We are all affected, more or less, by these thought forces, either consciously or unconsciously; and in the degree that we are more or less sensitively organized, or in the degree that we are negative and so are open to outside influences, rather than positive, thus determining what influences shall enter into our realm of thought, and hence into our lives.

There are those among us who are much more sensitively organized than others. As an organism their bodies are more finely, more sensitively constructed. These, generally speaking, are people who are always more or less affected by the mentalities of those with whom they come in contact, or in whose company they are.

Some think it unfortunate for one to be sensitively organized. By no means. It is a good thing, for one may thus be more open and receptive to the higher impulses of the soul within, and to all higher forces and influences from without. It may, however, be unfortunate and extremely inconvenient to be so organized unless one recognize and gain the power of closing himself, of making himself positive to all detrimental or undesirable influences. This power everyone, however sensitively organized he may be, can acquire.

This he can acquire through the mind's action. And, moreover, there is no habit of more value to anyone, be he sensitively or less sensitively organized, than that of occasionally taking and holding himself continually in the attitude of mind—I close myself, I make myself positive to all things below, and open and receptive to all higher influences, to all things above. By taking this attitude of mind consciously now and then, it soon becomes a habit, and if one is deeply in earnest in regard to it, it puts into operation silent but subtle and powerful influences in effecting the desired results. In this way all lower and undesirable influences from both the seen and the unseen side of life are closed out, while all higher influences are invited, and in the degree that they are invited will they enter.

Says one who knows full well whereof he speaks: "The law of attraction works universally on every plane of *action*, and we attract whatever we desire or expect. If we desire one thing and expect another, we become like houses divided against themselves, which are quickly brought to desolation. Determine resolutely to expect only what you desire, then you will attract only what you wish for. . . . Carry any kind of thought you please about with you, and so long as you retain it, no matter how you roam over land or sea, you will unceasingly attract to yourself, knowingly or inadvertently, exactly and only what corresponds to your own dominant quality of thought. Thoughts are our private property, and we can regulate them to suit our taste entirely by steadily recognizing our ability so to do."

We have just spoken of the drawing power of mind. Faith is nothing more nor less than the operation of the *thought forces* in the form of an earnest desire, coupled with expectation as to its fulfillment. And in the degree that faith, the earnest desire thus sent out, is continually held to and watered by firm expectation, in just that degree does it either draw to itself, or does it change from the unseen into the visible, from the spiritual into the material, that for which it is sent.

Let the element of doubt or fear enter in, and what would otherwise be

a tremendous force will be so neutralized that it will fail of its realization. Continually held to and continually watered by firm expectation, it becomes a force, a drawing power, that is irresistible and absolute, and the results will be absolute in direct proportion as it is absolute.

CHAPTER FOUR

Fullness of Life—
Bodily Health and Vigor

God is the Spirit of Infinite Life. If we are partakers of this life, and have the power of opening ourselves fully to its divine inflow, it means more, so far as even the physical life is concerned, than we may at first think. For very clearly, the life of this Infinite Spirit, from its very nature, can admit of no disease; and if this is true, no disease can exist in the body where it freely enters, through which it freely flows.

Let us recognize at the outset that, so far as the physical life is concerned, *all life is from within out.* There is an immutable law which says: "As within, so without; cause, effect." In other words, the thought forces, the various mental states and the emotions, all have in time their effects upon the physical body.

Someone says: "I hear a great deal said today in regard to the effects of the mind upon the body, but

I don't know as I place very much confidence in this." Don't you? Someone brings you sudden news. You grow pale, you tremble, or perhaps you fall into a faint. It is, however, through the channel of your mind that the news is imparted to you. A friend says something to you, perhaps at the table, something that seems very unkind. You are hurt by it, as we say. You have been enjoying your dinner, but from this moment your appetite is gone. But what was said entered into and affected you through the channel of your mind.

Again, a sudden emergency arises. You stand trembling and weak with fear. Why are you powerless to move? Why do you tremble? And yet you believe that the mind has but little influence upon the body. You are for a moment dominated by a fit of anger. For a few hours afterwards you complain of a violent headache. And still you do not seem to realize that the thoughts and emotions have an effect upon the body.

Fear and worry have the effect of closing up the channels of the body, so that the life forces flow in a slow and sluggish manner. Hope and tranquility open the channels of the body, so that the life forces go bounding through it in such a way that disease can rarely get a foothold.

I am aware of the fact that in connection with the matter we are now considering there has been a great deal of foolishness during the past few years. Many absurd and foolish things have been claimed and done; but this says nothing against, and it has absolutely nothing to do with, the great underlying laws themselves. The same has been true of the early days of practically every system of ethics or philosophy or religion the world has ever known. But as time has passed, these foolish, absurd things have fallen away, and the great eternal principles have stood out ever more and more clearly defined.

I know *personally* of many cases where an entire and permanent cure has been effected, in some within a remarkably short period of time, through the operation of these forces. Some of them are cases that had been entirely given up by the regular practice, *materia medica*. We have numerous accounts of such cases in all times and in connection with all religions. And why should not the power of effecting such cures exist among us today? The *power does exist*, and it will be actualized in just the degree that we recognize the same great laws that were recognized in times past.

The whole of human life is cause and effect; there is no such thing in it as chance, nor is there even in all the wide universe. Are we not satisfied with whatever comes into our lives? The thing to do, then, is not to spend time in railing against the imaginary something we create and call fate, but to look to the within, and change the causes at work there, in order that things of a different nature may come, for there will come exactly what we cause to come. This is true not only of the physical body, but of all phases and conditions of life.

The time will come when the work of the physician will not be to treat and attempt to heal the body, but to heal the mind, which in turn will heal the body. In other words, the true physician will be a teacher; his work will be to keep people well, instead of attempting to make them well after sickness and disease comes on; and still beyond this there will come a time when each will be his own physician. In the degree that we live in harmony with the higher laws of our being, and so, in the degree that we become better acquainted with the powers of the mind and spirit, will we give less attention to the body,—no less *care*, but less *attention*.

The bodies of thousands today would be much better cared for if their owners gave them less thought and attention. As a rule, those who think least of their bodies enjoy the best health. Many are kept in continual ill health by the abnormal thought and attention they give them.

Give the body the nourishment, the exercise, the fresh air, the sunlight it requires, keep it clean, and then think of it as little as possible. In your thoughts and in your conversation never dwell upon the negative side. Don't talk of sickness and disease. By talking of these you do yourself harm and you do harm to those who listen to you. Talk of those things that will make people the better for listening to you. Thus you will infect them with health and strength and not with weakness and disease.

To dwell upon the negative side is always destructive. This is true of the body the same as it is true of all other things.

The whole matter may then be summed up in the one sentence, "God is well and so are you." You must awaken to the knowledge of your *real being*. When this awakening comes, you will have, and you will see that you have, the power to determine what conditions are externalized in your body. You must recognize, you must realize yourself as one with Infinite Spirit. God's will is then your will; your will is God's will, and "with God all things are possible."

Chapter Five

Wisdom and Interior Illumination

If you would find the highest, the fullest, and the richest life that not only this world but that any world can know, then do away with the sense of the separateness of your life from the life of God. Hold to the thought of your oneness. In the degree that you do this you will find yourself realizing it more and more, and as this life of realization is lived, you will find that no good thing will be withheld, for all things are included in this. Then it will be yours, without fears or forebodings, simply to do today what your hands find to do, and so be ready for tomorrow, *when it comes*, knowing that tomorrow will bring tomorrow's supplies for the mental, the spiritual, and the physical life. Remember, however, that tomorrow's supplies are not needed until tomorrow comes.

If one is willing to trust himself *fully* to the Law, the Law will never fail him. It is the half-hearted trusting to it that brings uncertain, and so, unsatisfactory results. Nothing is firmer and surer than Deity. It will never fail the one who throws himself wholly upon it. The secret of life then, is to live continually in this realization, whatever one may be doing, wherever one may be, by day and by night, both waking and sleeping. It can be lived in while we are sleeping no less than when we are awake. And here shall we consider a few facts in connection with sleep, in connection with receiving instruction and illumination while asleep?

During the process of sleep it is merely the physical body that is at rest and in quiet; the soul life with all its activities goes right on. Sleep is nature's provision for the recuperation of the body, for the rebuilding and hence the replacing of the waste that is continually going on during the waking hours. It is nature's great restorer. If sufficient sleep is not allowed the body, so that the rebuilding may equalize the wasting process, the body is gradually depleted and weakened, and any ailment or malady, when it is in this condition, is able to find a more ready entrance. It is for this reason that those who are subject to it will take a cold, as we term it, more readily when the body is tired or exhausted through loss of sleep than at most any other time. The body is in that condition where outside influences can have a more ready effect upon it, than when it is in its normal condition. And when they do have an effect they always go to the weaker portions first.

Our bodies are given us to serve far higher purposes than we ordinarily use them for. Especially is this true in the numerous cases where the body is master of its owner. In the degree that we come into the realization of the higher powers of the mind and spirit, in that degree does the body, through their influence upon it, become less gross and heavy, finer in its texture and form. And then, because the mind finds a kingdom of enjoyment in itself, and in all the higher things it becomes related to, *excesses* in eating and drinking, as well as all others, naturally and of their own accord fall away. There also falls away the desire for the heavier, grosser, less valuable kinds of food and drink, such as the flesh of animals, alcoholic drinks, and all things of the class that stimulate the body and the passions rather than build the body and the brain into a strong, clean, well-nourished, enduring, and fibrous condition. In the degree that the body thus becomes less gross and heavy, finer in its texture and form, is there less waste, and what there is is more easily replaced, so that it keeps in a more regular and even condition. When this is true, less sleep is actually required. And even the amount that is taken does more for a body of this finer type than it can do for one of the other nature.

As the body in this way grows finer, in other words, as the process of its evolution is thus accelerated, it in turn helps the mind and the soul in the realization of ever higher perceptions, and thus body helps mind the same as mind builds body. It was undoubtedly this fact that Browning had in mind when he said:

> Let us cry "All good things
> Are ours, nor soul helps flesh, more now,
> Than flesh helps soul."

Sleep, then, is for the resting and the rebuilding of the body. The soul needs no rest, and while the body is at rest in sleep the soul life is active the same as when the body is in activity.

There are some, having a deep insight into the soul's activities, who say that we travel when we sleep. Some are able to recall and bring over into the conscious, waking life the scenes visited, the information gained, and the events that have transpired. Most people are not able to do this and so much that might otherwise be gained is lost. They say, however, that it is in our power, in proportion as we understand the laws, to go where we will, and to bring over into the conscious, waking life all the experiences thus gained. Be this, however, as it may, it certainly is true that while sleeping we have the power, in a perfectly normal and natural way, to get much of value by way of light, instruction, and growth that the majority of people now miss.

If the soul life, that which relates us to Infinite Spirit, is always active, even while the body is at rest, why may not the mind so direct conditions as one falls asleep, that while the body is at rest, it may continually receive illumination from the soul and bring what it thus receives over into the conscious, waking life? This, indeed, can be done, and is done by some to great advantage; and many times the highest inspirations from the soul come in this way, as would seem most natural, since at this time all communications from the outer, material world no longer enter. I know those who do much work during sleep, the same as they get much light along desired lines. By charging the mind on going to sleep as to a particular time for waking, it is possible, as many of us know, to wake on the very minute. Not infrequently we have examples of difficult problems, problems that defied solution during waking hours, being solved during sleep.

A friend, a well-known journalist, had an extended newspaper article clearly and completely worked out for her in this way. She frequently calls this agency to her aid. She was notified by the managing editor one evening to have the article ready in the morning—an article requiring more than ordinary care, and one in which quite a knowledge of facts was required. It was a matter in connection with which she knew scarcely anything, and all her efforts at finding information regarding it seemed to be of no avail.

She set to work, but it seemed as if even her own powers defied her. Failure seemed imminent. Almost in desperation she decided to retire, and putting the matter into her mind in such a way that she would be able to receive the greatest amount of aid while asleep, she fell asleep and slept soundly until morning. When she awoke her work of the previous evening was the first thing that came into her mind. She lay quietly for a few minutes, and as she lay there, the article, completely written, seemed to stand before her mind. She ran through it, arose, and without dressing took her pen and transcribed it onto paper, literally acting simply as her own amanuensis.

The mind acting intently along a particular line will continue so to act until some other object of thought carries it along another line. And since in sleep only the body is in quiet while the mind and soul are active, then the mind on being given a certain direction when one drops off to sleep, will take up the line along which it is directed, and can be made, in time, to bring over into consciousness the results of its activities. Some will be able very soon to get results of this kind; for some it will take longer. Quiet and continued effort will increase the faculty.

Then by virtue of the law of the drawing power of mind, since the mind is always active, we are drawing to us even while sleeping, influences from the realms kindred to those in which we in our thoughts are living before we fall asleep. In this way we can put ourselves into relation with whatever kinds of influence we choose and accordingly gain much during the process of sleep. In many ways the interior faculties are more open and receptive while we are in sleep than while we are awake. Hence the necessity of exercising even greater care as to the nature of the thoughts that occupy the mind as we enter into sleep, for there can come to us only what we by our own order of thought attract. We have it entirely in our own hands.

And for the same reason—this greater degree of receptivity during this period—we are able by under-standing and using the law, to gain much of value more readily in this way than when the physical senses are fully open to the material world about us. Many will find a practice somewhat after the following nature of value: When light or information is desired along any particular line, light or information you feel it is right and wise for you to have, as, for example, light in regard to an uncertain course of action, then as you retire, first bring your mind into the attitude of peace and goodwill for all. You in this way bring yourself into an harmonious condition, and in turn attract to yourself these same peaceful conditions from without.

Then resting in this sense of peace, quietly and calmly send out your earnest desire for the needed light or information; cast out of your mind all fears or forebodings lest it come not, for "in quietness and in confidence shall be your strength." Take the expectant attitude of mind, firmly believing and expecting that when you awake the desired results will be with you. Then on awaking, before any thoughts or activities from the outside world come in to absorb the attention, remain for a little while receptive to the intuitions or the impressions that come. When they come, when they manifest themselves clearly, then act upon them without delay. In the degree that you do this, in that degree will the power of doing it ever more effectively grow.

Or, if for unselfish purposes you desire to grow and develop any of your faculties, or to increase the health and strength of your body, take a corresponding attitude of mind, the form of which will readily suggest itself in accordance with your particular needs or desires. In this way you will open yourself to, you will connect yourself with, and you will set into operation within yourself, the particular order of forces that will make for these results. Don't be afraid to voice your desires. In this way you set into operation vibratory forces which go out and which make their impress felt somewhere, and which, arousing into activity or uniting with other forces, set about to actualize your desires. No good thing shall be withheld from him who lives in harmony with the higher laws and forces. There are no desires that shall not be satisfied to the one who knows and who wisely uses the powers with which he or she is endowed.

Your sleep will be more quiet and peaceful and refreshing, and so your power increased mentally, physically, and spiritually, simply by sending out as you fall asleep, thoughts of love and goodwill, thoughts of peace and harmony for all. In this way you are connecting yourself with all the forces in the universe that make for peace and harmony.

Visions and inspirations of the highest order will come in the degree that we make for them the right conditions.

When one awakes from sleep and so returns to conscious life, he is in a peculiarly receptive and impressionable state. All relations with the material world have for a time been shut off, the mind is in a freer and more natural state, resembling somewhat a sensitive plate, where impressions can readily leave their traces. This is why many times the highest and truest impressions come to one in the early morning hours, before the activities of the day and their attendant distractions have exerted an influence. This is one reason why many people can do their best work in the early hours of the day.

But this fact is also a most valuable one in connection with the molding of everyday life. The mind is at this time as a clean sheet of paper. We can most valuably use this quiet, receptive, impressionable period by wisely directing the activities of the mind along the highest and most desirable paths, and thus, so to speak, set the pace for the day.

Each morning is a fresh beginning. We are, as it were, just beginning life. We have it *entirely* in our own hands. And when the morning with its fresh beginning comes, all yesterdays should be yesterdays, with which we have nothing to do. Sufficient is it to know that the way we lived our yesterday has determined for us our today. And, again, when the morning with its fresh beginning comes, all tomorrows should be tomorrows, with which we have nothing to do. Sufficient to know that the way we live our today determines our tomorrow.

CHAPTER SIX

The Realization
of Perfect Peace

To recognize the fact that we are spirit, and to live in this thought, is to be spiritually minded, and so to be in harmony and peace. Oh, the thousands of men and women all about us weary with care, troubled and ill at ease, running hither and thither to find peace, weary in body, soul, and mind; going to other countries, traveling the world over, coming back, and still not finding it. Of course they have not found it and they never will find it in this way, because they are looking for it where it is not. They are looking for it without when they should look within. Peace is to be found only within, and unless one find it there he will never find it at all.

The moment we fear anything we open the door for the entrance of the actualization of the very thing we fear. An animal will never harm a person who is absolutely fearless in regard to it. The instant he fears he opens himself to danger; and some animals, the dog for example, can instantly detect the element of fear, and this gives them the courage to do harm. In the degree that we come into a full realization of our oneness with this Infinite Power do we become calm and quiet, undisturbed by the little occurrences that before so vex and annoy us. We are no longer disappointed in people, for we always read them aright. We have the power of penetrating into their very souls and seeing the underlying motives that are at work there.

A gentleman approached a friend the other day, and with great show of cordiality grasped him by the hand and said, "Why, Mr. _____, I am so glad to see you." Quick as a flash my friend read him, and looking him steadily in the eye, replied, "No, you are mistaken, you are not glad to see me; but you are very much disconcerted, so much so that you are now blushing in evidence of it." The gentleman replied, "Well, you know in this day and age of conventionality and form we have to put on the show and sometimes make believe what we do not really feel." My friend once more looked him in the face and said, "Again you are mistaken. Let me give you one little word of advice: You will always fare better and will think far more of yourself, always to recognize and to tell the truth rather than to give yourself to any semblance of it."

As soon as we are able to read people aright we will then cease to be disappointed in them, we will cease to place them on pedestals, for this can never be done without some attendant disappointment. The fall will necessarily come, sooner or later, and moreover, we are thus many times unfair to our friends. When we come into harmony with this Spirit of Peace, evil reports and apparent bad treatment, either at the hands of friends or of enemies, will no longer disturb us. When we are conscious of the fact that in our life and our work we are true to that eternal principle of right, of truth, of justice that runs through all the universe, that unites and governs all, that always eventually prevails, then nothing of this kind can come nigh us, and come what may we will always be tranquil and undisturbed.

The things that we open ourselves to always come to us. People in the olden times expected to see angels and they saw them; but there is no more reason why they should have seen them than that we should see them now; no more reason why they should come and dwell with them than that they should come and dwell with us, for the great laws governing all things are the same today as they were then. If angels come not to minister unto us it is because we do not invite them, it is because we keep the door closed through which they otherwise might enter.

In the degree that we are filled with this Spirit of Peace by thus opening ourselves to its inflow does it pour through us, so that we carry it with us wherever we go. In the degree that we thus open ourselves do we become magnets to attract peace from all sources; and in the degree that we attract and embody it in ourselves are we able to give it forth to others. We can in this way become such perfect embodiments of peace that wherever we go we are continually shedding benedictions.

Within each one lies the cause of whatever comes to him. Each has it in his own hands to determine what comes. Everything in the visible, material world has its origin in the unseen, the spiritual, the thought world. This is the world of cause, the former is the world of effect. The nature of the effect is always in accordance with the nature of the cause. What one lives in his invisible, thought world, he is continually actualizing in his visible, material world. If he would have any conditions different in the latter he must make the necessary change in the former. A clear realization of this great fact would bring success to thousands of men and women who all about us are now in the depths of despair. It would bring health, abounding health and strength to thousands now diseased and suffering. It would bring peace and joy to thousands now unhappy and ill at ease.

And oh, the thousands all about us who are continually living in the slavery of fear. The spirits within that should be strong and powerful are rendered weak and impotent. Their energies are crippled, their efforts are paralyzed. "Fear is everywhere—fear of want, fear of starvation, fear of public opinion, fear of private opinion, fear that what we own today may not be ours tomorrow, fear of sickness, fear of death. Fear has become with millions a fixed habit. The thought is everywhere. The thought is thrown upon us from every direction. . . . To live in continual dread, continual cringing, continual fear of anything, be it loss of love, loss of money, loss of position or situation, is to take the readiest means to lose what we fear we shall."

By fear nothing is to be gained, but on the contrary, everything is to be lost. "I know this is true," says one, "but I am given to fear; it's natural to me and I can't help it." Can't help it! In saying this you indicate one great reason of your fear by showing that you do not even know yourself as yet. You must know yourself in order to know your powers, and not until you know them can you use them wisely and fully. Don't say you can't help it. If you think you can't, the chances are that you can't. If you think you can, and act in accordance with this thought, then not only are the chances that you can, but if you act fully in accordance with it, that you can and that you will is an absolute certainty. It was Virgil who in describing the crew which in his mind would win the race, said of them—They can because they think they can. In other words, this very attitude of mind on their part will infuse a spiritual power into their bodies that will give them the strength and endurance which will enable them to win.

Then take the thought that you *can*; take it merely as a seed-thought, if need be, plant it in your consciousness, tend it, cultivate it, and it will gradually reach out and gather strength from all quarters. It will focus and make positive and active the spiritual force within you that is now scattered and of little avail. It will draw to itself force from without. It will draw to your aid the influence of other minds of its own nature, minds that are fearless, strong, courageous. You will thus draw to yourself and connect yourself with this order of thought. If earnest and faithful, the time will soon come when all fear will loose its hold; and instead of being an embodiment of weakness and a creature of circumstances, you will find yourself a tower of strength and a master of circumstances.

Materialism leads naturally to pessimism. And how could it do otherwise? A knowledge of the Spiritual Power working in and through us as well as in and through all things, a power that works for righteousness, leads to optimism. Pessimism leads to weakness.

Optimism leads to power. The one who is centered in Deity is the one who not only outrides every storm, but who through the faith, and so, the conscious power that is in him, faces storm with the same calmness and serenity that he faces fair weather; for he knows well beforehand what the outcome will be.

CHAPTER SEVEN

Coming Into Fullness of Power

This is the Spirit of Infinite Power, and in the degree that we open ourselves to it does power become manifest in us. With God all things are possible—that is, in conjunction with God all things are possible. The true secret of power lies in keeping one's connection with the God who worketh all things; and in the degree that we keep this connection are we able literally to rise above every conceivable limitation.

Why, then, waste time in running hither and thither to acquire power? Why waste time with this practice or that practice? Why not go directly to the mountain top itself, instead of wandering through the byways, in the valleys, and on the mountain sides? That man has absolute dominion, as taught in all the scriptures of the world, is true not of physical man, but of *spiritual man.* There are many animals, for example, larger and stronger, over which from a physical standpoint he would not have dominion, but he can gain supremacy over even these by calling into activity the higher mental, psychic, and spiritual forces with which he is endowed.

Whatever can't be done in the physical can be done in the spiritual. And in direct proportion as a man recognizes himself as spirit, and lives accordingly, is he able to transcend in power the man who recognizes himself merely as material. All the sacred literature of the world is teeming with examples of what we call miracles. They are not confined to any particular times or places. There is no age of miracles in distinction from any other period that may be an age of miracles. Whatever has been done in the world's history can be done again through the operation of the same laws and forces. These miracles were performed not by those who were more than men, but by those who through the recognition of their oneness with God became God-men, so that the higher forces and powers worked through them.

For what, let us ask, is a miracle? Is it something supernatural? Supernatural only in the sense of being above the natural, or rather above that which is natural to man in his ordinary state. A miracle is nothing more nor less than this. One who has come into a knowledge of his true identity, of his oneness with the all-pervading Wisdom and Power, thus makes it possible for laws higher than the ordinary mind knows of to be revealed to him. These laws he makes use of; the people see the results, and by virtue of their own limitations, call them miracles and speak of the person who performs these apparently supernatural works as a supernatural being. But they as supernatural beings could themselves perform these supernatural works if they would open themselves to the recognition of the same laws, and consequently to the realization of the same possibilities and powers.

And let us also remember that the supernatural of yesterday becomes, as in the process of evolution we advance from the lower to the higher, from the more material to the more spiritual, the common and the natural of today, and what seems to be the supernatural of today becomes in the same way the natural of tomorrow, and so on through the ages. Yes, it is the God-man who does the things that appear supernatural, the man who by virtue of his realization of the higher powers transcends the majority and so stands out among them. But any power that is possible to one human soul is possible to another. The same laws operate in every life. We can be men and women of power or we can be men and women of impotence. The moment one vitally grasps the fact that he can rise he will rise, and he can have absolutely no limitations other than the limitations he sets to himself. Cream always rises to the top. It rises simply because *it is the nature of cream to rise.*

We hear much said of "environment." We need to realize that environment should never be allowed to make the man, but that man should always, *and always can*, condition the environment. When we realize this we will find that many times it is not necessary to take ourselves out of any particular environment, because we may yet have a work to do there; but by the very force we carry with us we can so affect and change matters that we will have an entirely new set of conditions in an old environment.

The same is true in regard to "hereditary" traits and influences. We sometimes hear the question asked, "Can they be overcome?" Only the one who doesn't yet know himself can ask a question such as this. If we entertain and live in the belief that they cannot be overcome, then the chances are that they will always remain. The moment, however, that we come into a realization of our true selves, and so of the tremendous powers and forces within—the powers and forces of the mind and spirit—hereditary traits and influences that are harmful in nature will begin to lessen, and will disappear with a rapidity directly in proportion to the completeness of this realization.

Again there are many who are living far below their possibilities because they are continually handing over their individualities to others. Do you want to be a power in the world? Then be yourself. Don't class yourself, don't allow yourself to be classed among the second-hand, among the *they-say* people. Be true to the highest within your own soul, and then allow yourself to be governed by no customs or conventionalities or arbitrary man-made rules that are not founded upon *principle*. Those things that are founded upon principle will be observed by the right-minded, the right-hearted man or woman, in any case.

Don't surrender your individuality, which is your greatest agent of power, to the customs and conventionalities that have gotten their life from the great mass of those who haven't enough force to preserve their individualities—those who in other words have given them over as ingredients to the "mush of concession" which one of our greatest writers has said characterizes our modern society. If you do surrender your individuality in this way, you simply aid in increasing the undesirable conditions; in payment for this you become a slave, and the chances are that in time you will be unable to hold even the respect of those whom you in this way try to please.

If you preserve your individuality then you become a master, and if wise and discreet, your influence and power will be an aid in bringing about a higher, a better, and a more healthy set of conditions in the world. All people, moreover, will think more of you, will honor you more highly for doing this than if you show your weakness by contributing yourself to the same "mush of concession" that so many of them are contributing themselves to. With all classes of people you will then have an influence. "A great style of hero draws equally all classes, all extremes of society to him, till we say the very dogs believe in him."

To be one's self is the only worthy, and by all means the only satisfactory, thing to be. "May it not be good policy," says one, "to be governed sometimes by one's surroundings?" What is good policy? To be yourself, first, last, and always.

The men and the women who are truly awake to the real powers within are the men and women who seem to be doing so little, yet who in reality are doing so much. They seem to be doing so little because they are working with higher agencies, and yet are doing so much because of this very fact. They do their work on the higher plane. They keep so completely their connection with the Infinite Power that *It* does the work for them and they are relieved of the responsibility. They are the care-less people. They are care-less because it is the Infinite Power that is working through them, and with this Infinite Power they are simply cooperating.

The secret of the highest power is simply the uniting of the outer agencies of expression with the Power that works from within.

I had rather be an amanuensis of the Infinite God, as it is my privilege literally to be, than a slave to the formulated rules of any rhetorician, or to the opinions of any critic. Oh, the people, the people over and over! Let me give something to them that will lighten the everyday struggles of our common life, something that will add a little sweetness here, a little hope there, something that will make more thoughtful, kind, and gentle this thoughtless, animal-natured man, something that will awaken into activity the dormant powers of this timid, shrinking little woman, powers that when awakened will be irresistible in their influence and that will surprise even herself. Let me give something that will lead each one to the knowledge of the divinity of every human soul, something that will lead each one to the conscious realization of *his own divinity*, with all its attendant riches, and glories, and powers—let me succeed in doing this, and I can then well afford to be careless as to whether the critics praise or whether they blame. If it is blame, then under these circumstances it is as the cracking of a few dead sticks on the ground below, compared to the matchless music that the soft spring gale is breathing through the great pine forest.

If when born into the world you came into a family of the English-speaking race, then in all probability you are a Christian. To be a Christian is to be a follower of the *teachings* of Jesus, the Christ; to live in harmony with the same laws he lived in harmony with: in brief, *to live his life*. The great central fact of his teaching was this conscious union of man with the Father. It was the complete realization of this oneness with the Father on his part that made Jesus the Christ. It was through this that he attained to the power he attained to, that he spake as never man spake.

He never claimed for himself anything that he did not claim equally for all mankind. "The mighty works performed by Jesus were not exceptional, they were the natural and necessary concomitants of his state; he declared them to be in accordance with unvarying order; he spoke of them as no unique performances, but as the outcome of a state to which all might attain if they chose. As a teacher and demonstrator of truth, according to his own confession, he did nothing for the purpose of proving his solitary divinity. . . . The life and triumph of Jesus formed an epoch in the history of the race. His coming and victory marked a new era in human affairs; he introduced a new because a more complete ideal to the earth, and when his three most intimate companions saw in some measure what the new life really signified, they fell to the earth, speechless with awe and admiration."

By coming into this complete realization of his oneness with the Father, by mastering, absolutely mastering every circumstance that crossed his path through life, even to the death of the body, and by pointing out to us the great laws which are the same for us as they were for him, he has given us an ideal of life, an ideal for us to attain to *here and now*, that we could not have without him. *One has conquered first; all may conquer afterward.* By completely realizing it first for himself, and then by pointing out to others this great law of the at-one-ment with the Father, he has become probably the world's greatest savior.

Don't mistake his mere person for his life and his teachings, an error that has been made in connection with most all great teachers by their disciples over and over again. And if you have been among the number who have been preaching a dead Christ, then for humanity's sake, for Christ's sake, for God's sake, and I speak most reverently, don't steal the people's time any longer, don't waste your own time more, in giving them stones in place of bread, dead form for the spirit of living truth. In his own words, "let the dead bury their dead." Come out from among them. Teach as did Jesus, *the living Christ*. Teach as did Jesus, *the Christ within*. Find this in all its transcendent beauty and power— find it as Jesus found it, then you also will be one who will speak with authority. Then you will be able to lead large numbers of others to its finding. This is the pearl of great price.

CHAPTER EIGHT

Plenty of All Things— The Law of Prosperity

This is the Spirit of Infinite Plenty, the Power that has brought, that is continually bringing, all things into expression in material form. He who lives in the realization of his oneness with this Infinite Power becomes a magnet to attract to himself a continual supply of whatsoever things he desires.

If one hold himself in the thought of poverty, he will be poor, and the chances are that he will remain in poverty. If he hold himself, whatever present conditions may be, continually in the thought of prosperity, he sets into operation forces that will sooner or later bring him into prosperous conditions. The law of attraction works unceasingly throughout the universe, and the one great and never-changing fact in connection with it is, as we have found, that like attracts like. If we are one with this Infinite Power, this source of all things, then in the degree that we live in the realization of this oneness, in that degree do we actualize in ourselves a power that will bring to us an abundance of all things that it is desirable for us to have. In this way we come into possession of a power whereby we can actualize at all times those conditions that we desire.

As all truth exists *now*, and awaits simply our perception of it, so all things necessary for present needs exist *now*, and await simply the power in us to appropriate them. God holds all things in His hands. His constant word is, My child, acknowledge me in all your ways, and in the degree that you do this, in the degree that you live this, then what is mine is yours. Jehovah-jireh—the Lord will provide. "He giveth to all men liberally and upbraideth not." He giveth liberally to all men who put themselves in the right attitude to receive from Him. He forces no good things upon any one.

The old and somewhat prevalent idea of godliness and poverty has absolutely no basis for its existence, and the sooner we get away from it the better. It had its birth in the same way that the idea of asceticism came into existence, when the idea prevailed that there was necessarily a warfare between the flesh and the spirit. It had its origin therefore in the minds of those who had a distorted, a one-sided view of life. True godliness is in a sense the same as true wisdom. The one who is truly wise, and who uses the forces and powers with which he is endowed, to him the great universe always opens her treasure house. The supply is always equal to the demand—equal to the demand when the demand is rightly, wisely made. When one comes into the realization of these higher laws, then the fear of want ceases to tyrannize over him.

Are you out of a job? Let the fear that you will not get another take hold of and *dominate* you, and the chances are that it may be a long time before you will get another, or the one that you do get may be a very poor one indeed. Whatever the circumstances, you must realize that you have within you forces and powers that you can set into operation that will triumph over any and all apparent or temporary losses. Set these forces into operation and you will then be placing a magnet that will draw to you a situation that may be far better than the one you have lost, and the time may soon come when you will be even thankful that you lost the old one.

Recognize, working in and through you, the same Infinite Power that creates and governs all things in the universe, the same Infinite Power that governs the endless systems of worlds in space. Send out your thought—thought is a force, and it has occult power of unknown proportions when rightly used and wisely directed—send out your thought that the right situation or the right work will come to you at the right time, in the right way, and that you will recognize it when it comes. Hold to this thought, never allow it to weaken, hold to it, and continually water it with firm expectation. You in this way put your advertisement into a psychical, a spiritual newspaper, a paper that has not a limited circulation, but one that will make its way not only to the utmost bounds of the earth, but of the very universe itself. It is an advertisement, moreover, which if rightly placed on your part, will be far more effective than any advertisement you could possibly put into any printed sheet, no matter what claims are made in regard to its being "the great advertising medium." In the degree that you come into this realization and live in harmony with the higher laws and forces, in that degree will you be able to do this effectively.

If you wish to look through the "want" columns of the newspapers, then do it not in the ordinary way. Put the higher forces into operation and thus place it on a higher basis. As you take up the paper, take this attitude of mind: If there is here an advertisement that it will be well for me to reply to, the moment I come to it I will recognize it. Affirm this, believe it, expect it. If you do this in full faith you will somehow feel the intuition the moment you come to the right one, and this intuition will be nothing more nor less than your own soul speaking to you. When it speaks then act at once.

If you get the job and it does not prove to be exactly what you want, if you feel that you are capable of filling a better one, then the moment you enter upon it take the attitude of mind that this situation is the steppingstone that will lead you to one that will be still better. Hold this thought steadily, affirm it, believe it, expect it, and all the time be faithful, *absolutely faithful* to the situation in which you are at present placed. If you are *not* faithful to it then the chances are that it will not be the steppingstone to something better, but to something poorer. If you are faithful to it, the time may soon come when you will be glad and thankful, when you will rejoice, that you lost your old position.

This is the law of prosperity: When apparent adversity comes, be not cast down by it, but make the best of it, and always look forward for better things, for conditions more prosperous. To hold yourself in this attitude of mind is to set into operation subtle, silent, and irresistible forces that sooner or later will actualize in material form that which is today merely an idea. But ideas have occult power, and ideas, when rightly planted and rightly tended, are the seeds that actualize material conditions.

Never give a moment to complaint, but utilize the time that would otherwise be spent in this way in looking forward and actualizing the conditions you desire. Suggest prosperity to yourself. See yourself in a prosperous condition. Affirm that you will before long be in a prosperous condition. Affirm it calmly and quietly, but strongly and confidently. Believe it, believe it absolutely. Expect it—keep it continually watered with expectation. You thus make yourself a magnet to attract the things that you desire. Don't be afraid to suggest, to affirm these things, for by so doing you put forth an ideal which will begin to clothe itself in material form. In this way you are utilizing agents among the most subtle and powerful in the universe. If you are particularly desirous for anything that you feel it is good and right for you to have, something that will broaden your life or that will increase your usefulness to others, simply hold the thought that at the right time, in the right way, and through the right instrumentality, there will come to you or there will open up for you the way whereby you can attain what you desire.

I know of a young lady who a short time ago wanted some money very badly. She wanted it for a good purpose; she saw no reason why she shouldn't have it. She is one who has come into an understanding of the power of the interior forces. She took and held herself in the attitude of mind we have just pointed out. In the morning she entered into the silence for a few moments. In this way she brought herself into a more complete harmony with the higher powers. Before the day closed a gentleman called, a member of a family with which she was acquainted. He asked her if she would do for the family some work that they wanted done. She was a little surprised that they should ask her to do this particular kind of work, but she said to herself, "Here is a call. I will respond and see what it will lead to." She undertook the work. *She did it well*. When she had completed it there was put into her hands an amount of money far beyond what she had expected. She felt that it was an amount too large for the work she had done. She protested. They replied, "No; you have done us a service that transcends in value the amount we offer to pay you." The sum thus received was more than sufficient for the work she wished to accomplish.

This is but one of many instances in connection with the wise and effective use of the higher powers. It also carries a lesson,—Don't fold your hands and expect to see things drop into your lap, but set into operation the higher forces and then take hold of the first thing that offers itself. Do what your hands find to do, *and do it well*. If this work is not thoroughly satisfactory to you, then affirm, believe, and expect that it is the agency that will lead you to something better. "The basis for attracting the best of all the world can give to you is to first surround, own, and live in these things in mind, or what is falsely called imagination. All so-called imaginings are realities and forces of unseen element. Live in mind in a palace and gradually palatial surroundings will gravitate to you. But so living is *not* pining, or longing, or complainingly wishing. It is when you are 'down in the world,' calmly and persistently seeing yourself as up. It is when you are now compelled to eat from a tin plate, regarding that tin plate as only the certain step to one of silver. It is not envying and growling at other people who have silver plate. That growling is just so much capital stock taken from the bank account of mental force."

A friend who knows the power of the interior forces, and whose life is guided in every detail by them, has given a suggestion in this form: When you are in the arms of the bear, even though he is hugging you, look him in the face and laugh, but all the time keep your eye on the bull. If you allow all of your attention to be given to the work of the bear, the bull may get entirely out of your sight. In other words, if you yield to adversity the chances are that it will master you, but if you recognize in yourself the power of mastery over conditions then adversity will yield to you, and will be changed into prosperity. If when it comes you calmly and quietly recognize it, and use the time that might otherwise be spent in regrets, and fears, and forebodings, in setting into operation the powerful forces within you, it will soon take its leave.

Faith, absolute dogmatic faith, is the only law of true success. When we recognize the fact that a man carries his success or his failure with him, and that it does not depend upon outside conditions, we will come into the possession of powers that will quickly change outside conditions into agencies that make for success. When we come into this higher realization and bring our lives into complete harmony with the higher laws, we will then be able so to focus and direct the awakened interior forces, that they will go out and return laden with that for which they are sent. We will then be great enough to attract success, and it will not always be apparently just a little ways ahead. We can then establish in ourselves a center so strong that instead of running hither and thither for this or that, we can stay at home and draw to us the conditions we desire. If we firmly establish and hold to this center, things will seem continually to come our way.

The one who has come into the realization of the higher life no longer has a desire for the accumulation of enormous wealth, any more than he has a desire for any other *excess*. In the degree that he comes into the recognition of the fact that he is wealthy within, external wealth becomes less important in his estimation. When he comes into the realization of the fact that there is a source within from which he can put forth a power to call to him and actualize in his hands at any time a sufficient supply for all his needs, he no longer burdens himself with vast material accumulations that require his constant care and attention, and thus take his time and his thought from the real things of life. In other words, he first finds the *kingdom*, and he realizes that when he has found this, all other things follow in full measure.

It is as hard for a rich man to enter into the kingdom of heaven, said the Master—he who having nothing had everything—as it is for a camel to pass through the eye of a needle. In other words, if a man give all his time to the accumulation, the hoarding of outward material possessions far beyond what he can possibly ever use, what time has he for the finding of that wonderful kingdom, which when found, brings all else with it. Which is better, to have millions of dollars, and to have the burden of taking care of it all—for the one always involves the other—or to come into the knowledge of such laws and forces that every need will be supplied in good time, to know that no good thing shall be withheld, to know that we have it in our power to make the supply always equal to the demand?

Wealth beyond a certain amount cannot be used, and when it cannot be used it then becomes a hindrance rather than an aid, a curse rather than a blessing. There is no wiser use that those who have great accumulations can make of them than wisely to put them into life, into character, *day by day while they live.* In this way their lives will be continually enriched and increased. The time will come when it will be regarded as a disgrace for a man to die and leave vast accumulations behind him.

Chapter Nine

How Men Have Become Prophets, Seers, Sages, and Saviors

All the prophets, seers, sages, and saviors in the world's history became what they became, and consequently had the powers they had, through an entirely natural process. They all recognized and came into the conscious realization of their oneness with the Infinite Life. God is no respecter of persons. He doesn't create prophets, seers, sages, and saviors as such. He creates men. But here and there one recognizes his true identity, recognizes the oneness of his life with the Source whence it came. He lives in the realization of this oneness, and in turn becomes a prophet, seer, sage, or savior. Neither is God a respecter of races or of nations. He has no chosen people; but here and there a race or nation becomes a respecter of God and hence lives the life of a chosen people.

There has been no age or place of miracles in distinction from any other age or place. What we term miracles have abounded in all places and at all times where conditions have been made for them. They are being performed today just as much as they ever have been when the laws governing them are respected. Mighty men, we are told they were, mighty men who walked with God; and in the words "who walked with God" lies the secret of the words "mighty men." Cause, effect.

The Lord never prospers any man, but the man prospers because he acknowledges the Lord, and lives in accordance with the higher laws. Solomon was given the opportunity of choosing whatever he desired; his better judgment prevailed and he chose wisdom. But when he chose wisdom he found that it included all else beside. We are told that God hardened Pharaoh's heart. I don't believe it. God never hardens any one's heart. Pharaoh hardened his own heart and God was blamed for it. But when Pharaoh hardened his heart and disobeyed the voice of God, the plagues came. Again, cause, effect. Had he, on the contrary, listened—in other words, had he opened himself to and obeyed the voice of God, the plagues would not have come.

We can be our own best friends or we can be our own worst enemies. In the degree that we become friends to the highest and best within us, we become friends to all; and in the degree that we become enemies to the highest and best within us, do we become enemies to all. In the degree that we open ourselves to the higher powers and let them manifest through us, then by the very inspirations we carry with us do we become in a sense the saviors of our fellow-men, and in this way we all are, or may become, the saviors one of another. In this way you may become, indeed, one of the world's redeemers.

CHAPTER TEN

The Basic Principle of all Religions—The Universal Religion

The great truth we are considering is the fundamental principle running through all religions. We find it in everyone. In regard to it all agree. It is, moreover, a great truth in regard to which all people can agree, whether they belong to the same or to different religions. People always quarrel about the trifles, about their personal views of minor insignificant points. They always come together in the presence of great fundamental truths, the threads of which run through all. The quarrels are in connection with the lower self, the agreements are in connection with the higher self.

A place may have its factions that quarrel and fight among themselves, but let a great calamity come upon the land, flood, famine, pestilence, and these little personal differences are entirely forgotten and all work shoulder to shoulder in the one great cause. The changing, the evolving self gives rise to quarrels; the permanent, the soul-self unites all in the highest efforts of love and service.

Patriotism is a beautiful thing; it is well for me to love my country, but why should I love my own country more than I love all others? If I love my own and hate others, I then show my limitations, and my patriotism will stand the test not even for my own. If I love my own country and in the same way love all other countries, then I show the largeness of my nature, and a patriotism of this kind is noble and always to be relied upon.

The view of God in regard to which we are agreed, that He is the Infinite Spirit of Life and Power that is back of all, that is working in and through all, that is the life of all, is a matter in regard to which all men, all religions can agree. With this view there can be no infidels or atheists. There are atheists and infidels in connection with many views that are held concerning God, and thank God there are. Even devout and earnest people among us attribute things to God that no respectable men or women would permit to be attributed to themselves. This view is satisfying to those who cannot see how God can be angry with his children, jealous, vindictive. A display of these qualities always lessens our respect for men and women, and still we attribute them to God.

The earnest, sincere heretic is one of the greatest friends true religion can have. Heretics are among God's greatest servants. They are among the true servants of mankind. Christ was one of the greatest heretics the world has ever known. He allowed himself to be bound by no established or orthodox teachings or beliefs. Christ is preëminently a type of the universal. John the Baptist is a type of the personal. John dressed in a particular way, ate a particular kind of food, belonged to a particular order, lived and taught in a particular locality, and he himself recognized the fact that he must decrease while Christ must increase. Christ, on the other hand, gave himself absolutely no limitations. He allowed himself to be bound by nothing. He was absolutely universal and as a consequence taught not for his own particular day, but for all time.

This mighty truth which we have agreed upon as the great central fact of human life is the golden thread that runs through all religions. When we make it the paramount fact in our lives we will find that minor differences, narrow prejudices, and all these laughable absurdities will so fall away by virtue of their very insignificance, that a Jew can worship equally as well in a Catholic cathedral, a Catholic in a Jewish synagogue, a Buddhist in a Christian church, a Christian in a Buddhist temple. Or all can worship equally well about their own hearthstones, or out on the hillside, or while pursuing the avocations of everyday life. For true worship, only God and the human soul are necessary. It does not depend upon times, or seasons, or occasions.

Anywhere and at any time God and man in the bush may meet.

This is the great fundamental principle of the universal religion upon which all can agree. This is the great fact that is permanent. There are many things in regard to which all cannot agree. These are the things that are personal, nonessential, and so as time passes they gradually fall away. One who doesn't grasp this great truth, a Christian, for example, asks "But was not Christ inspired?" Yes, but he was not the only one inspired. Another who is a Buddhist asks, "Was not Buddha inspired?" Yes, but he was not the only one inspired. A Christian asks, "But is not our Christian Bible inspired?" Yes, but there are other inspired scriptures. A Brahmin or a Buddhist asks, "Are not the Vedas inspired?" Yes, but there are other inspired sacred books. Your error is not in believing that your particular scriptures are inspired, but your error is—and you show your absurdly laughable limitations by it—your inability to see that other scriptures are also inspired.

The sacred books, the inspired writings, all come from the same source—God, God speaking through the souls of those who open themselves that He may thus speak. Some may be more inspired than others. It depends entirely on the relative degree that this one or that one opens himself to the Divine voice. Says one of the inspired writers in the Hebrew scriptures, Wisdom is the breath of the power of God, and *in all ages* entering into holy souls she maketh them friends of God and prophets.

The great fundamental principles of all religions are the same. They differ only in their minor details according to the various degrees of unfoldment of different people. I am sometimes asked, "To what religion do you belong?" What religion? Why, bless you, there is only one religion—the religion of the living God. There are, of course, the various creeds of the same religion arising from the various interpretations of different people, but they are all of minor importance. The more unfolded the soul the less important do these minor differences become. There are also, of course, the various so-called religions. There is in reality, however, but one religion.

Chapter Eleven

Entering Now Into the Realization of the Highest Riches

I hear the question, What can be said in a concrete way in regard to the method of coming into this realization? The facts underlying it are, indeed, most beautiful and true, but how can we actualize in ourselves the realization that carries with it such wonderful results?

The method is not difficult if we do not of ourselves make it difficult. The principal word to be used is the word—Open. Simply to open your mind and heart to this divine inflow which is waiting only for the opening of the gate, that it may enter. It is like opening the gate of the trough which conducts the water from the reservoir above into the field below. The water, by virtue of its very nature, will rush in and irrigate the field if the gate is but opened. As to the realization of our oneness with this Infinite Life and Power, after seeing, as I think we have clearly seen by this time, the relations it bears to us and we to it, the chief thing to be said is simply— Realize your oneness with it. The open mind and heart whereby one is brought into the receptive attitude is the first thing necessary. Then the earnest, sincere desire.

It may be an aid at first to take yourself for a few moments each day into the quiet, into the silence, where you will not be agitated by the disturbances that enter in through the avenues of the physical senses. There in the quiet alone with God, put yourself into the receptive attitude. Calmly, quietly, and expectantly desire that this realization break in upon and take possession of your soul. As it breaks in upon and takes possession of the soul, it will manifest itself to your mind, and from this you will feel its manifestations in every part of your body. Then in the degree that you open yourself to it you will feel a quiet, peaceful, illuminating power that will harmonize body, soul, and mind, and that will then harmonize these with all the world. You are now on the mountain top, and the voice of God is speaking to you. *Then, as you descend, carry this realization with you*. Live in it, waking, working, thinking, walking, sleeping. In this way, although you may not be continually on the mountain top, you will nevertheless be continually living in the realization of all the beauty, and inspiration, and power you have felt there.

Moreover, the time will come when in the busy office or on the noisy street you can enter into the silence by simply drawing the mantle of your own thoughts about you and realizing that there and everywhere the Spirit of Infinite Life, Love, Wisdom, Peace, Power, and Plenty is guiding, keeping, protecting, leading you. This is the spirit of continual prayer. This it is to pray without ceasing. This it is to know and to walk with God. *This it is to find the Christ within*. This is the new birth, the second birth. First that which is natural, then that which is spiritual. It is thus that the old man Adam is put off and the new man Christ is put on. This it is to be saved unto life eternal, whatever one's form of belief or faith may be; for it is life eternal to know God. "The Sweet By and By" will be a song of the past. We will create a new song—"The Beautiful Eternal Now."

This is the realization that you and I can come into this very day, this very hour, this very minute, if we desire and if we will it. And if now we merely set our faces in the right direction, it is then but a matter of time until we come into the full splendors of this complete realization. To set one's face in the direction of the mountain and then simply to journey on, whether rapidly or more slowly, will bring him to it. But unless one set his face in the right direction and make the start, he will not reach it. It was Goethe who said:

> *Are you in earnest? Seize this very minute:*
> *What you can do, or dream you can, begin it;*
> *Boldness has genius, power, and magic in it.*
> *Only engage and then the mind grows heated;*
> *Begin and then the work will be completed.**

Said the young man, Gautama Siddhârtha, I have awakened to the truth and I am resolved to accomplish my purpose—Verily I shall become a Buddha. It was this that brought him into the life of the Enlightened One, and so into the realization of Nirvana right here in this life. That this same realization and life is within the possibilities of all here and now was his teaching. It was this that has made him the Light Bearer to millions of people.

Said the young man, Jesus, Know ye not that I must be about my Father's business? Making this the one great purpose of his life he came into the full and complete realization—I and the Father are one. He thus came into the full realization of the Kingdom of Heaven

---

* Trine is quoting a very loose 1835 translation of Goethe's *Faust* by Irish poet John Anster.—MH

right here in this life. That all could come into this same realization and life here and now was his teaching. It was this that has made him the Light Bearer to millions of people.

And so far as practical things are concerned, we may hunt the wide universe through and we shall find that there is no injunction more practical than, Seek ye first the kingdom of God and His righteousness and all other things shall be added unto you. And in the light of what has gone before, I think there is no one who is open to truth and honest with himself who will fail to grasp the underlying reason and see the great laws upon which it is based.

As one comes into and lives continually in the full, conscious realization of his oneness with the Infinite Life and Power, then all else follows. This it is that brings the realization of such splendors, and beauties, and joys as a life that is thus related with the Infinite Power alone can know. This it is to come into the realization of heaven's richest treasures while walking the earth. This it is to bring heaven down to earth, or rather to bring earth up to heaven. This it is to exchange weakness and impotence for strength; sorrows and sighings for joy; fears and forebodings for faith; longings for realizations. This it is to come into fullness of peace, power, and plenty. This it is to be in tune with the Infinite.

Chapter Twelve

"The Way"

Life is not so complex if we do not so persistently make it so. We accept the results or the effects; but we concern ourselves all too little with the realm of cause. The springs of life are all from within. Invariably it is true—as is the inner so always and inevitably will be the outer.

There is a Divine current that will bear us with peace and safety on its bosom if we are sufficiently alert and determined to find it and go with it. The natural, normal life is by a law divine under the guidance of the Spirit.

There is a mystic force that transcends the powers of the intellect and likewise of the body. There are certain faculties that we have that are not a part of the active, thinking mind; they transcend any possible activities of the active, thinking mind. Through them we have intuitions, impulses, leadings, that instead of being merely the occasional, *should be the normal and habitual.*

They would be if we understood better the laws that pertain to them and observed them; for here, as in connection with everything in the universe and everything in human life, all is governed by law—the Elemental law of cause and effect. Supreme Intelligence, Creative Power, works only through law. There is an inner spirit or guide that rules and regulates the life when the life is brought into that state or condition whereby it can make itself known, and in turn dominate the life.

Jesus, Master of the laws of life, and supreme revealer of them to men, had a full and practical knowledge of it. He not only abundantly demonstrated it in His own life; but He made clear the way whereby it may become the common possession of other lives. Do not worry about your life, was the Master's clear-cut and repeated command. He not only gave the injunction or command, but He demonstrated the method whereby the fears and forebodings and uncertainties of life can be displaced by a force or a power that will bring them to an end.

It was embodied in His other injunction or command that He gave utterance to so repeatedly: "Seek ye first the Kingdom of God and His righteousness and all these things shall be added to you." And by all these things, He meant, all of the common needs and necessities of the daily life.

The finding of the Kingdom of God is the recognition of the indwelling Divine Life as the source, and therefore as the Essence, of our own lives. It is the bringing of men's minds and therefore acts into harmony with the Divine will and purpose. It is the saving of men from their lower conceptions and selves, and a lifting them up to a realization of their higher selves, which, as He taught, is eternally one with God, the Father; and which, when realized, lifts a man's thoughts, acts, purposes, and conduct—his entire life—up to that pattern or standard.

It was not merely a poetic fancy, but the recognition of a fundamental law, as well-known laws of modern psychology, mental and spiritual science, are now clearly demonstrating, that induced the Master to say: "And thine ears shall hear a word behind thee, saying, This is the way, walk ye in it, when ye turn to the righthand and when ye turn to the left." And again: "The Lord in the midst of thee is mighty." And still again: "He that dwelleth in the secret place of the Most High shall abide under the shadow of the Almighty."

How often do the meager accounts of the Master's life tell us of His going up to the mountain to pray—*for communion with the Father*. And then we find Him invariably down among men, always where the need for help and for human service was the greatest.

This habit of taking a little time daily alone, in the quiet, in communion with one's Source that the illumination and guidance of the Holy Spirit may become alive and active in the life, and going then about one's daily work ever open to and conscious of this Divine guidance, trusting and resting in it, strengthened and sustained always by this Divine power, will bring definiteness and direction, will bring hope and courage, will bring peace and power to everyone who will heed the Master's injunction and will follow His example. These it has brought to great numbers to whom before, life was an enigma, and this because the life had been lived entirely from the outside.

The higher forces and powers of the inner life, those of the mind and spirit, always potential within, become of actual value only as they are recognized, realized, and used.

The Master's *Way of the Spirit*, the finding of the Kingdom within, leads into no blind alley. It leads out and triumphantly out onto the great plain of clear vision, of un-self-centered activity, of heroic endeavor and accomplishment.

If we would spend a fraction of the time that we spend in needless anxiety in definite constructive thought, in "silent demand," visualizing the conditions that we would have, with faith in their fulfillment, we would soon know that the Master's illustration of the carefree bird is fact and not fancy. It is, He said, what life should be.

The little time spent in the quiet each day, alone with one's God, that we may make and keep our connection with the Infinite Source, "our source and our life," will be a boon to any life. It will prove, if we are faithful, to be the most priceless possession that we have.

While it is impossible for one to make a formula which another should follow, the following may perchance contain some little suggestions—each must follow his or her own leading and, therefore, method.

My Father in Heaven, Infinite Spirit of life and love and wisdom and power, in whom I live and move and have my being, whence cometh my help, manifest Thyself in me.

Help me to open myself to the highest wisdom and insight and love and power, that I may serve Thee and my fellow-man, and all my fellow-creatures faithfully, and that I may have the Divine guidance and care, and that all my needs be supplied.

Oh *Christ within*, enfold and lead me and reign supreme, that the One Life that is my life I may realize and manifest ever more fully.

I am strong in the Infinite Spirit of life and love and wisdom and power. I have and shall have the Divine guidance and care; for it is the Father that worketh in me—My Father works and I work.

The following little motto—a resolve for today—may contain a little aid for the following of the *Way*.

I AM RESOLVED

I believe that my Master intended that I take His teachings in the simple, frank, and open manner in which He gave them, out on the hillside, by the calm blue waters of the Galilean sea, and out under the stars of heaven.

I believe that He knew what He meant, and that He meant what He said, when He gave the substance of all religion and the duty of man as love to God, and love and service for His fellow-men.

I am therefore resolved at this, the beginning of another day, this fresh beginning of life, to go forth eager and happy and unafraid,

*in that I can come into the same filial relations
of love and guidance and care with my Father
in Heaven that my Master realized and lived,
and going before revealed to me.*

*I shall listen intently to know, and shall
run with eager feet to do my Father's will, calm
and quiet within, knowing that I shall have the
Divine guidance and care, and that no harm
therefore shall befall me; for I am now living in
God's life and there I shall live forever.*

*I am resolved in all human contact to meet
petulance with patience, questionings with
kindness, hatred with love, eager always to do
the kindly deed that brings the joy of service—
and that alone makes human life truly human.*

*I shall seek no advantage for myself to the
detriment or the harm of my neighbor, knowing
that it is only through the law of mutuality that
I can fully enjoy what I gain—or can even be a
man.*

*I am resolved therefore so to live this day
that, when the twilight comes and the night
falls, I shall be not only another day's journey
nearer home; but I shall have lived a man's part
and done a man's work in the world and shall
indeed deserve my Father's love and care.*

About the Authors

A pioneering figure in the New Thought movement and one of the most popular voices in American metaphysics, RALPH WALDO TRINE was born in 1866 in Mount Morris, Illinois. The author of more than a dozen books, Trine began working as a journalist before writing his classic *In Tune With the Infinite* in 1897, which went on to sell more than two million copies and inspired a generation of spiritual and motivational writers. He died in Claremont, California, in 1958.

MITCH HOROWITZ is the PEN Award-winning author of books including *Occult America* and *The Miracle Club*. Mitch introduces and edits G&D Media's line of Condensed Classics and is the author of the Napoleon Hill Success Course series including *The Miracle of a Definite Chief Aim* and *Secrets of Self Mastery*. Twitter: @MitchHorowitz | Instagram: @MitchHorowitz23

Printed in the USA
CPSIA information can be obtained
at www.ICGtesting.com
JSHW012042140824
68134JS00033B/3222